OVERVIEW

This idea pulls from the resources, statistics, and issues from my previous publication Heir to the Invisible Throne Syndrome: Sports Development and the American Dream. Binding Heir to the Invisible Throne Syndrome (H.I.T.S) and The Need for Social Workers in Sport for Development (N.S.W.S.D). This is a theoretical idea of a perfect functioning social work and sport for development environment through Sport Life Association of Betterment (SLAB) that will provide Sport Life Betterment Coaches to athletes at all universities and possibly on a professional level. **S.L.A.B**: derived from the method of creating shapes in pottery. Slab Method of making pottery in which a thick, flat plate, or slice, of clay is cut into shapes which are joined to form an object. Social work and sport for development are the objects that needs to join forces to create slab method athletes who are able to handle their pressurized environment and to have a better after sports life. It is time to join the pieces.

ACKNOWLEDGEMENTS

I would like to say thank you to my sons Tristan and Tevers Brittingham for giving me my undeniable ambition and strength. Tristan Brittingham for his critique and criticism. Kanika Reese of Peerless Publications for editing, and Ernestine Cook Jones, Eds. for editing assistance and encouragement.

ABSTRACT

Athletes face a plethora of dilemmas related to socio-economics, family dynamics, poverty, mental health, pressure to win, pressure to succeed, pressure to provide for the family, mental and emotional abuse, physical abuse, sexual abuse, substance abuse, bullying, absent parenting, discrimination, and many other psychosocial issues, but are still expected to perform at high levels without mandatory psychosocial professional support. There is a tremendous need for a greater social worker presence on college/school campuses. All student athletes should be assigned a Life Betterment Coach (social worker) to address pending stressful issues. Research, funding, and implementation of programs such as the Sport Life Association of Betterment that will provide Sport Life Betterment Coaches to athletes that will positively affect sport participation for generations to come. The objective of this research is to prove that such a program is needed and a stronger social worker presence in sports development will better the life of athletes in schools and colleges.

INTRODUCTION

Athletes are expected to appear larger than life, absent of all other emotions and problems that regular people endure. They are our heroes and expected to be heroes and nothing less than a hero. Any athlete that shows signs of being less than a hero with supernatural abilities and absent of regular human emotions are often ridiculed or publicly shamed for his/her behavior. National Alliance of Social Workers in Sports (NASWIS) was recently created to address the needs of athletes and underserved populations within the athletic community. The NASWIS (2017) mission is to help with development, improve character, and ensure individual resilience, due to the recent increase in exploitation of athletes at all levels of sports. The National Basketball Association (NBA) has developed their own mental health wellness program funded by the league and union, due to various social problems professional athletes grapple with in their daily lives (Aldridge, 2018). The program is said to include a rookie transitioning program, team awareness program, and player assistance program confronting mental illness, stress, attention, and constant demands for money (Aldridge, 2018). It is my observation that it is time that the all state high school athletic organizations, National Collegiate Athletic Association (NCAA) and all college institutions should come together to develop a major organization such a Sports Life Association of Betterment that will serve college athletes more extensively, during high school, after transition from high school and before transitioning into society or professional sports.

This study will show that a lack of social workers in all level of sports causes several catastrophic social disasters that are going under or are unaddressed such as: family problems, anxiety, discrimination, bullying, eating disorders, drug abuse, stress, and various other issues. This study will show that a stronger social worker presence in sports can focus on issues such as coping with common problems, building character, identify and address mental health problems, social issues, success outside of sports, and advocate for research, case management and counseling. Social workers in sports development offers advocacy, case coordination, counseling, and program and policy changes that are needed to serve such a vulnerable population of people. Social workers in sports development would address mental health issues, a better after sports life, nuclear family problems, societal changes, institutional changes (mandatory graduation assurance for all collegiate athletes, NCAA policy changes, etc.), support and counseling while competing.

School and collegiate athletes deal with the same problems on different scales and various magnitudes. Throughout this research there will be scholarly references supporting youth athletes and collegiate athletes' issues and the need for more social workers in both aspects of sports. Hermens and colleagues (2017) research supports that social workers used as facilitators and barrier breakers would transcend sport participation and reduce stressors that socially vulnerable student athletes face in everyday life such as: stressors from income poverty, unhealthy lifestyles, feelings of incompetence and rejection, and negative experiences with institutions such as the family and school (Hermens, et al., 2017). Social workers in place as co-organizers in sports would allow for successful coordination action between school, universities, and families. Hermens and associates (2017) previously found research indicating that coordinated actions improve community outcomes, build new relationships, and provide proper procedure and structure for crisis intervention and individual coping skills. Each person or entity associated with an athlete has a different aim. Parents, coaches, universities, school athlete programs, peer groups of athletes have different goals, visions, plans, and expectations of the athlete. However, a social worker would be a frontline member that would be able to bridge the gap and dismantle social barriers between the athlete and their multiple social group dynamics. Social work services in sports development would directly affect athletes experiencing complications in their personal development, which is often due to learning or behavioral obstacles or because lack proper care emotionally (Hermens, et al., 2017).

It has been argued that there are latent benefits in sports such as structure and socialization. Also, sports can influence development, self-esteem, leadership skills, positive socialization, and teamwork skills (Brown, et al., 2011). When athletes are faced with innumerable amounts of social and ecological challenges they tend to seek out sports as a cure-all for life challenges, which can lead to questionable ethics and unrealistic goal setting (Brown, et al., 2011). Literature that connects athletics and social work rarely exist, but it is often suggested that social workers in athletics can explore the social and ecological challenges of athletes as a determining principle for positive development (Brown, et al., 2011). Social workers are well suited to handle any and all issues regarding social service in athletics because social workers often seek to work with "underserved populations, provide an ethical barometer to professional approaches to well-being, and have multiple methods of addressing social and emotional concerns (Brown, et al., 2011)." Athletes are not generally thought of as being underserved or what people in society considers to be "in need." In my opinion, the lack of social workers available to collegiate athletes and maybe one counselor or social worker available to a school with thousands of children is a precise definition of underserved. We need to change our view on what underserved means, it does not always mean "poor" monetarily, but poorly taken care of and easily disposed. When problems such as mental health, drug and substance abuse, discrimination, anxiety, family pressures and dynamics, stress, and eating disorders amongst athletes are brushed under the rug and not addressed head, this on is a strong indication that athletes are extensively underserved. We should no longer dispose of our athletes when they are not winning and earning millions for school program. My analysis is that social work is an emerging sector in sports development and there are some colleges with mental health professionals in place to help students. However, as impossible as this project may appear theoretically; I hope to prove that a program such as Sports Life Association of Betterment can be successfully implemented and that Sports Life Betterment Coaches are needed in vast numbers in schools and colleges to curtail the problems school and collegiate athletes face.

PURPOSE, AIM, GOAL, AND HYPOTHESES

The purpose of this study would be to prove that there is a need for each athlete to be assigned a social worker as an early intervention method of addressing social problems in athletics for sports development: to counsel, mentor, and identify family issues, help with transitioning to college life, help with a better after college life; help athletes with understanding statistical odds of making it as a professional athlete, help athletes develop coping skills to deal with pressure; identifying mental health, drug and substance abuse problems, anxiety, stress, discrimination, and various other problems that may surface. Possible hypotheses to be tested: (1) Compared with students-athletes who have had some form of counseling, mental health treatment, or any preventative service, to student athlete with no preventative measure have high rates of negative mental states or high rates of negative after college life exist. (2) Student athletes with unaddressed emotional, social, and mental health problems will experience more negative impacts in their athletic career and collegiate after life. (3) Compare student athletes with assigned social workers to student athletes with no social services in place are more likely to have a better social, mental, and emotional collegiate experience resulting in a better during and after sports life. (4) Social workers can be positive catalysts for a positive collaboration between athletes, coaches, institutions, and families for improvements in sports development.

AIM AND GOAL

The aim of this study is to investigate the need for more social workers to be assigned to athletes for promotion, prevention, and early intervention of issues collegiate athletes endure. In the world of athletics, players feel pressured to appear perfect. The inclusion of assigned social workers will allow players to be more upfront and willing to tackle emotional, mental, and social problems that they have been conditioned to feel that those things make them imperfect.

RESEARCH QUESTIONS

The research would propose the following question along with sample demographic questions such as: year in school (first, second, third, fourth), age, race/ethnicity, gender, sexuality.

Measuring the lack and need of social worker services and student experience with these questions:

1. Have you ever felt hopeless?

2. Have you ever felt very lonely?

3. Have you had a hard time transitioning into college life and athletes?

4. Have you ever felt so depressed that it was difficult to function?

5. Have you received any social services by a professional to address emotional, mental, or social problems and needs?

6. Have you ever felt overwhelming anxiety?

7. Have you ever felt overwhelming anger?

8. Have you ever felt emotionally unstable or emotionally out of control?

9. Have you ever felt that the pressure to stay fit has caused eating problems?

10. Have you ever felt discriminated against because of your race, gender, or ethnicity as a student athlete?

11. Have you ever felt as though you needed additional counseling outside of your coaches?

12. Have you ever felt bullied by teammates?

13. Have you felt overwhelmed by family dynamics (economic status, pressure, broken relationships, etc.)

14. Have you used drugs and alcohol?

15. Have you ever felt pressure to use alcohol or drugs of any kind?

16. Have you ever felt that your coach would not understand your anxiety, family problems, anger, depression, or stress?

17. Do you feel that you need a direct professional contact to help with emotional, mental, or social problem, needs?

18. Have you wanted or felt you needed the help of a social service professional, but felt ashamed to ask for help?

19. If a social service professional was in place such as a social worker, do you feel that service would reduce or help cope with personal issues in collegiate athletic setting?

20. Would you take advantage of having an assigned social worker?

SIGNIFICANCE OF THE PROBLEM

There are several who oppose the position sports take in an athlete's life. Brown and colleagues (2011) found that non-sports fans and those who do not believe in the basic foundation of sports such as character building, feel as though sports promote aggression, callousness, violence, militarism, can be emotionally and philosophically abusive with high levels of parental misconduct. To date, there is no conclusive research that shows an importance of the relationship between sport and social intervention. The resilience of research continues to try to prove that social workers and social services is the missing key and buffer needed between stress, trauma, family, the coach, the institution, and the sport. Brown and colleagues (2011) discovered that sports programs that provide social workers or social services properly can provide athletes with structure and emotional safety allowing room for present and future healing and growth. Social work can be used in team sports as an ally in the promotion of social groupwork and as an effective intervention. In my opinion, in order to conclusively prove that social workers are needed in sports, and that social workers in sports development should be enacted as an intervention method tackling trauma, anger and aggression, social and emotional learning, coping skills, and discipline can be done effectively, if social workers are provided on a collegiate/school level to all athletes, while utilizing sports intervention group practices when planning and implementing care. This type of research beginning with middle school through college can lead to development of best practices for all in athletics (coaches, administrators, family, athletes, institutions, etc.) concerned with and affected by social and emotional learning and character development.

My analysis is that social service sport-based intervention can be used as a quintessential complementary service of treatment in athletics. As professionals we are often confined to rigid ways of thinking and not allowed to "think outside the box" when it comes to treatment and intervention methods. However, social workers in sports development will have a positive impact while promoting social work's core values of service, social justice, dignity and worth of the person, the importance of human relationships, integrity, and competence (NASW, 2017) and

(Brown et al., 2011). Schools and collegiate institutions should seize the opportunity to implement social services on campus attacking athletic social and mental limitations and focusing on strengthening and supporting athletes to their fullest potential (Brown, et al., 2011).

STATEMENT OF PURPOSE

How the times have changed and things have progressed, it is evident that the sport alone is not enough to build character, when the sport causes various personal problems, and the problems of the athlete playing the sport is not considered. Sport focused intervention was constructed within a functionalist socialization model addressing the relationship between sports participation and character, morality, delinquency, academic performance, status, and politics (Crabbe, 2000). Those who have spent a majority of their lives playing a sport are greatly influenced by the activity. However, it is not possible to make the assumption that specific patterns of character development or behavior have a consistent pattern of change because of sports participation (Crabbe, 2000). This research will show that consistency and adequate intervention can only be done with implementation of a consistent social service program. I think that with the inclusion of social workers in sports development, problems student athlete struggle with such as: low self-esteem, social issues, stress, depression, and many other problems can be permanently addressed, evaluated, changed, improved, and built upon.

Athlete's behavior, mental state, family dynamics, coach relationship, economic problems, drug taking, violence, domestic violence, corruption, cheating, racism, homophobia, intimidation, sex scandals and other forms of criminal behavior will become increasingly uncertain, unpredictable, and unmanageable without the encompassment of social workers in sports development. However, it is possible to keep sport traditions and implement new ways successfully as long as the athlete and others involved are aware that such ideas can teach them something they think is worth knowing (Crabbe, 2000). Social workers in sports development should not be viewed as being a sports project, diversionary scheme or punitive measure. Social workers in sports development initiative is about "community development in a real sense, since it is about developing relationships with people on the basis of trust and mutual understanding as a platform for building a broader range of relationships and opportunities (Crabbe, 2000)." Crabbe's (2000) research was focus on using sports to tackle drug use and crime, but the information and findings are relevant to why a stronger social worker base is needed in athletics. I think that society may fear that the incorporation of social service will cause the "game" to lose the "fun factor" when servicing the importance of education, character development, or social improvement. However, servicing the mental, emotional, and social needs of collegiate athlete with the addition of social workers in sports would better the game, better the athlete, and better the system.

SIGNIFICANCE OF THE STUDY: A HOLISTIC ECOLOGICAL APPROACH PSYCHOSOCIAL DEVELOPMENT THEORY AND SYSTEMS THEORY

I am proposing that using holistic ecological approach to identify the need of a stronger social worker presence in sports development would bring about the realizations that there is an interlocking system between social workers and sports development. This study would help to reinforce the culture of psychosocial development and systems theory in sports development and confirm the correlation of psychosocial development and systems theory when involving social workers in sports development. Transitioning from one level in sports to another is one of the most difficult and complex transitions in sports (Larsen, Alfermann, Henriksen, & Christensen, 2014). Larsen and colleagues (2014) research states that a holistic approach to talent development in athletics would focus more on the athletic environment; using modern scientist practitioner model, the practitioner can be seen as a researcher who relies on theory to make assessments of a problem and decide the best strategies. Larsen and colleagues (2014) research confirms my proposal for the need to implement more social workers in sports as practitioners functioning from a holistic ecological perspective using primary theories such as psychosocial and systems theories to carry out the assessment process, along with social learning theory and rational choice theory. During the implementation process it would be important to use the following five social work practice models for treatment: problem solving, task-centered practice, narrative therapy, cognitive behavior therapy, and the crisis intervention model.

Lauren and colleagues (2014) successfully designed an intervention to strengthen athletes and the environment. It is my observation that if a greater social worker presence was enacted in athletics to help athletes transition from high school, to college, to society, or professional sports while addressing mental health and social needs, it would be as successful if the program followed through with the suggested steps of Lauren and colleagues (2014) listed below:

> " (1) the program and the social workers should acknowledge that the athlete is embedded in an environment by involve the athletes' environment (coaches, institutions, teammates etc.); (2) holistic perspective, thus looking into strengths and weaknesses in the organizational culture and the micro and macro environment in and out of the sporting domain; (3) practitioner (social worker) should not only work with the individual athletes, but aim to optimize the entire environment around the athlete or team; (4) creating a good dialogue among the environment's different agents; take this cultural setting into consideration and plan the intervention; (5) intervention should aim to create and maintain a strong and coherent organizational culture; (6) it is suggested that successful environments see the athletes as whole human beings and support the development of a holistic package of psychosocial skills that will be of use for the athletes not only in their sport, but indeed in their other life spheres as well."

Erik Erikson developed the psychosocial theory with the idea of focusing on the way individuals are shaped by and react to their social environment (Engard, 2017). The theory states that individuals sense of self grows and evolves as they come into contact with a series of social crises during a lifetime and each crisis forces the individual to react and adapt (Engard, 2017).

There are eight stages of the theory, that can be related to social crises such as: "trust versus mistrust, which occurs in infancy and informs how an individual trusts; industry versus inferiority, which informs qualities like work ethic, competency and self-worth; and intimacy versus isolation, which provides the basis for love (Engard, 2017)."

Erikson's Stages of Psychosocial Development

Approximate Age	Psycho Social Crisis
Infant - 18 months	Trust vs. Mistrust
18 months - 3 years	Autonomy vs. Shame & Doubt
3 - 5 years	Initiative vs. Guilt
5 -13 years	Industry vs. Inferiority
13 -21 years	Identity vs. Role Confusion
21- 39 years	Intimacy vs. Isolation
40 - 65 years	Generativity vs. Stagnation
65 and older	Ego Integrity vs. Despair

(C) The Psychology Notes Headquarter - http://www.PsychologyNotesHQ.com

Social crises inform "how individuals see themselves, how they react to the Erikson's psychosocial theory states that social crises informs us how individuals see themselves, how they react to the world and people around them, and what skills they develop in life (Engard, 2017). Engard (2017) suggested that social workers can use psychosocial theory as a "maturation timetable" to inform how they treat clients, types of services provided, and define how clients differ in treatment and expectations. My observation is that a holistic ecological approach guided by a psychosocial and systems theory, using the social work practice model as a means and methods of treatment, implementation would the foundation of practice when broadening the presence of social workers in sports development.

SOCIAL WORK THEORIES

Social work theories that would be beneficial in implementing a social work program based for college athletes as defined below by Simmons School of Social Work (2014):

Systems Theory

Defined as describing human behavior in terms of complex systems. It is premised on the idea that an effective system is based on individual needs, rewards, expectations, and attributes of the people living in the system. According to this theory, families, couples, and organization members are directly involved in resolving a problem even if it is an individual issue.

Social Learning Theory

Defined as being based on Albert Bandura's idea that learning occurs through observation and imitation, new behavior will continue if it is reinforced. According to this theory, rather than simply hearing a new concept and applying it, the learning process is made more efficient if the new behavior is modeled as well.

Rational Choice Theory

Defined as being based on the idea that all action is fundamentally rational in character, and people calculate the risks and benefits of any action before making decisions.

SOCIAL WORK PRACTICE MODEL

All social work model can be used as beneficial tools during the helping process as defined by Simmons School of Social Work (2014):

Problem Solving

Defined as it assists people with the problem-solving process. Rather than tell clients what to do, social workers teach clients how to apply a problem-solving method so they can develop their own solutions.

Task-centered Practice

Defined as a short-term treatment where clients establish specific, measurable goals. Social workers and clients collaborate together and create specific strategies and steps to begin reaching those goals.

Narrative Therapy

Defined as it externalizes a person's problem by examining the story of the person's life. In the story, the client is not defined by the problem, and the problem exists as a separate entity. Instead of focusing on a client's depression, in this social work practice model, a client would be encouraged to fight against the depression by looking at the skills and abilities that may have previously been taken for granted.

Cognitive Behavioral Therapy

Defined as it focuses on the relationship between thoughts, feelings, and behaviors. Social workers assist clients in identifying patterns of irrational and self-destructive thoughts and behaviors that influence emotions.

Crisis Intervention Model

Defined as it is used when someone is dealing with an acute crisis. The model includes seven stages: assess safety and lethality, rapport building, problem identification, addressing feelings, generating alternatives, developing an action plan, and following up. This social work practice model is commonly used with clients who are expressing suicidal ideation.

THE NEED FOR SPORT LIFE BETTERMENT COACHES

Athletes deal with the same issues as normal students previously mentioned such as: bullying, death of a family member, illness, oppression, poverty, discrimination, domestic violence, emotional neglect, absent parent, substance-abuse, etc. (Levenson, 2017). Campus social workers (Sport Life Betterment Coaches) can provide trauma-focused therapy with a primary goal of viewing present issues. Sport Life Betterment Coaches can be a driving force in an athletic department to convey respect, compassion, teach self-determination, rebuild healthy interpersonal skills and coping strategies (Levenson, 2017). "Social workers are trained to avoid over pathologizing behavior and to appreciate the complex nexus between poverty, oppression, and trauma (Levenson, 2017)."

Campus social workers can create a better environment for student athletes that will transition to a better after sports life. Social workers are able to understand how common trauma can be and that victimization in any form can affect psychosocial development and provide permanent coping skills (Levenson, 2017). College or school campus social workers would be able to focus more on building skills rather than addressing symptoms. Levenson (2017) study explains that this form of social work is beneficial when applied throughout intake, assessment, engagement, treatment, and termination phases of services. The purpose of campus social work would be to minimize dysfunctional dynamics and create corrective experiences (Levenson, 2017).

Social workers are tasked with helping those that lack basic human necessities, when thinking of the vulnerable, we tend to only think of those impoverished (Gill, 2008). Social work theorists, researchers, and practitioners often leave out college athletics or athletics in general; simply because student-athletes are not considered to be in need because of their physical ability, idea of privilege, and their short lived social status (Gill, 2008). College sports

recruit a vast majority of adolescents from hazardous environments where crime and gang

activity presides over a poor secondary education (Gill, 2008). Athletes are viewed as the elite;

yet, their vulnerability is overshadowed by field lights and collegiate prestige. African American

and International student-athletes often lack family support, community support, trusted role

models, while fighting student-athlete stereotypes and adapting to their new environment (Gill,

2008).

Gill (2008) describes the tragic story of Anthony Vontoure as stated below:

Vontoure, a cornerback with NFL talent, was dismissed from the football team after
frequent outbursts, uncontrollable anger, smashed windows, and conflicts with coaches.
On the evening of May 31,2002, while Vontoure was staying with a friend, the police
were summoned to the apartment because Vontoure said he was frightened that little
green men in masks wanted to kill him, and his roommates feared he was having a
nervous breakdown (Miller, 2002). University of Washington coaches and officials
claimed that Vontoure was diagnosed with a bipolar disorder, prescribed medication, and
saw counselors. To the contrary, his mother, who battled two bouts of depression, said
she was not informed of Anthony's diagnosis and saw no signs that he was on
medication. One coach surmised that Vontoure was off his medication when the AH-
America candidate shared he did not have any money. Five officers were needed to
restrain Vontoure, but after his breathing changed from rapid to shallow, he was
transported to a local medical center where he was pronounced dead. According to
Vontoure's geology professor, "I wasn't surprised something overcame him. He was
carrying an enormous weight."

Anthony Vontoure's story is an example of the imperative need of social work in athletics.

Student-athletes are not immune to life difficulties, mental health issues, financial problems; in

fact, they are at a greater risk for these issues particularly depression, anxiety, and substance

abuse. Gill (2008) research and findings show that social work is the most appropriate

profession to promote student-athlete development to fulfill an obvious hole in social service in

athletics and the community.

Sport participation is a badge of honor for American childhood and adolescence. On average "twenty-five million children and adolescents play competitive sports within schools and 30 to 45 million participate in at least one school or community-based athletic program" (Teasley and Gill, 2015). Student-athletes are able to thrive with proper mentorship such as time given, attention, and parent, teacher and coach contributions. Athletes who have a positive mentor earn higher grades, make better decisions, and experience better professional outcomes when compared to nonathletes (Teasley and Gill, 2015). Mentoring is an effective tool in youth sports support to students to help them manage a wide range of pressures and difficulties. However, some may argue that mentoring research is limited and assumed that anyone can be a mentor. Mentors who lack proper professional counseling and intervention skills are expected to deliver "miracle cures for what are deep-routed and multidimensional social problems." This argument confirms that there is a need to combine social work and sports development (Teasley and Gill, 2015). Sport Life Betterment Coaches functioning in a role of mentor and counselor would be the miracle cure Teasley and Gill (2015) in athletes.

Sport Life Association of Betterment and Sport Life Betterment Coaches

This is an example of how to implement Sport Life Betterment Coaches across collegiate and school systems using the cycle of policy research.

Social Work: Social Welfare Policy

Cycle of Policy Research

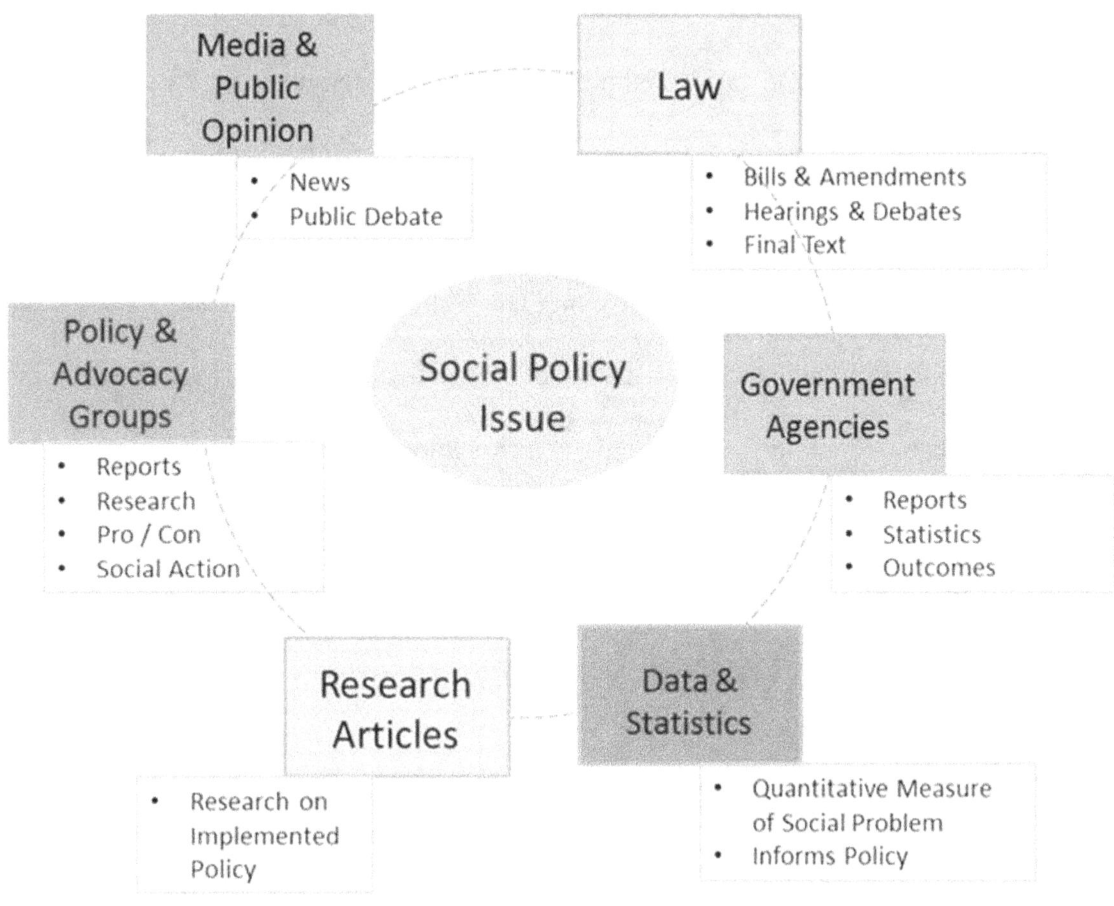

EXAMPLE OF METHOD: CORRELATION

This study would prove there is a strong positive correlation between social workers presence in sports and addressing mental health problems early, a better after sports life, increased counseling for nuclear family problems, societal changes, institutional changes (mandatory graduation assurance for all collegiate athletes, NCAA policy changes, etc.), support and counseling while competing. Convergent Validity: when there is more social worker presence in all aspects of sports education, awareness, family, injury, a better after sports life, and ethics.

Men, women, youth, and various ethnicities will face different struggles with equal pressures and demands. The common life obstacles of athletes include dealing with depression, anxiety, substance abuse, eating disorders, difficulty transitioning to new employment after an athletic career, cognitive issues, and chronic pain (The College of St. Scholastica, 2017). Social workers assist people from all backgrounds and ethnicities that are dealing with everyday life difficulties and crises. Generally, society tends to lack sympathy for athletes who struggle with daily life problems. A stronger social worker presence in sports can provide athletes with the support needed to cope with common problems, build character, identify and address mental health problems, social issues, success outside of sports, and advocate for research, case management and counseling.

Gaining a better understanding of professional ethics and modes of teaching ethics within coaching education is of critical importance (Thompson & Dieffenbach, 2016). Coaches are tremendously influential when it comes to the development of athletes. Social work can provide the need for increased opportunities for ethics. Education is an essential component of coach training (Thompson & Dieffenbach, 2016). Coaching is a complex profession with a variety of ethical dilemmas. As coaching education develops, it is critical to implement support training on professional ethics with the hopes of shaping the decision-making process into a positive one.

Parents, coaches, and the educational systems (high school and collegiate) are responsible for informing the student athlete about making sound career choices. A solid educational foundation is needed to build a successful career (Bertram, 2013). If the sports foundation (institutions, coaches, NCAA, social workers) and family foundation (parents and student athlete) work together, it will empower student athletes to set realistic dreams and pursue their own passions and hobbies (Bertram, 2013). There must be a plan B career and education plan in place of the plan A, the chance of making it pro; both plans must be worked at the same time. Education (math, science, etc.) should be placed ahead of sports at an early age. Student athletes must begin realistically and strategically thinking about their careers long before they finish high school (Bertram, 2013). Parents, coaches, and scholarly institutions must foster a curiosity and collaboration for critical thinking and problem-solving skills (Bertram, 2013). This responsibility should be placed on society as a whole and all professional sports leagues.

Athletes should continue to focus on team building skills, work ethics, leadership, and emotional control while participating in their selected sport, but most importantly, they must focus on preparing for the global economy ahead of them (Bertram, 2013). If scholarship possibilities are slim by the time the youth reaches late middle school age, parents should begin directing the youth's attention to decide on what other career possibilities are available, and seek out other passions. This is where an early form of school social work is needed to address career possibilities and future goals and endeavors. The child may have other dreams that he/she wants to achieve. Bertram (2013) confirms that campus social workers would be the guiding force between student athletes, coaches, parents, collegiate/school facilities, leagues, and counselors providing a bridge to psychosocial professional assistance in sports, intervening and introducing the athlete to other available career options, and guide them on the path to pursue those careers with the appropriate course work and activities.

IMPLEMENTATION PROCESS

This type of study if implemented should consist of a quantitative correlation study that analyze the statistical difference in athlete lives after an implementation of social workers assigned to athletes across multiple college campuses. It is possible to study one collegiate program to compare a reduction in mental health issues, family issues, after sports life, injury education, and a career back-up plan. There is no independent and dependent variable when using a correlation construct; however, statistical methods are one of two types: descriptive methods (that describe attributes of a data set) and inferential methods (that try to draw conclusions about a population based on sample data). Many correlated relationships between two measurement variables tend to fall close to a straight line. To analyze the statistics, it must be determined whether the correlation between variables is significant, compare the p-value to your significance level. Usually, a significance level (denoted as α or alpha) of 0.05 works well. An α of 0.05 indicates that the risk of concluding that a correlation exists—when, actually, no correlation exists—is 5%.

LITERATURE REVIEW:

COLLEGIATE STUDENT ATHLETE SOCIAL PROBLEMS

I have observed, over the past several years, that the sport itself is being over-shadowed by unresolved social problems such as: drug taking, violence, domestic violence, corruption, cheating, racism, homophobia, intimidation, sex scandals and other forms of criminal behavior. In sports news there are just as many reports of great achievements as there are reports of downfalls, tragedy, and social conflicts. The emergence of the abundance of complications shows that there is an unpropitious need for social services and social work in sports development. The social worker intervention must directly address characteristics that can be changed and that are associated with current obstacles in sports development (Crabbe, 2000). Sports have been the only aspect of social intervention because the sport itself should 'build character." Yet, society has not taken into account what it takes to maintain and empower the character.

Collegiate athletes have stressors and expectations of them unlike other students that can trigger or exacerbate mental health issues (Noren, 2014). Due to this factor, there has been a spark in interest in student athletes' mental health, therefore, the National Collegiate Athletic Association (NCAA) Mental Health Task Force (NCAA) has recently released a mental health handbook (Greville, 2014). Greville (2014) explained that transitioning from high school to college is a stressful process for athletes because of "demanding schedules, the distance from home, adjusting to a new level of academics, working with new teammates and coaches, and possibly suffering injuries, they often are underprepared to deal with these stressors because of underdeveloped coping mechanisms."

College athletes are burdened with pressures of being observed, judged, and ridiculed by peers, coaches, fans, parents, classmates, and teachers. Along with self-placed expectations fuels inevitable mental, social, and emotional problems for athletes. My observation is that these types of issues often lead to drug addiction, substance abuse, and mental health breakdowns. Collegiate athletes are not likely to admit these issues are a problem and are self-taught to push through and ignore the signs (Greville, 2014). Greville (2014) research found that student athletes do not seek help of social workers because they are determined to handle things on their own, but have been witnessed crying in their car after games and only seek help of an on campus social worker if the social worker reaches out. This is evident that social workers should be assigned to student athletes and college institutions should implement Sport Life Association of Betterment that will provide Sport Life Betterment Coaches to athletes will positively affect sport participation. As experts we should not sit back and wait for student athletes to ask for help. We are aware that there is a need for prevention and intervention at this level.

Greville (2014) determined that most colleges have an athletic counselor responsible for servicing the entire department social service needs. The University of Michigan athletics department employs licensed mental health professional that exclusively work with student athletes that are dealing with anxiety, depression, ADHD, and adjustment issues (Greville, 2014). I emphatically believe that one counselor cannot properly service an entire athletic department's social needs and coaches lack the professional knowledge and experience to handle such issues. Students are expected to seek help of the counselor on their own and often do not because they feel ashamed by the stigmas that come with seeking social service help because in sports that is viewed as "weak." Greville's (2014) research revealed that student athletes do not have adequate self-care skills, and the stigma of appearing weak presents a strong barrier. Treatment cannot be undervalued. This information has lead me to determine that the only way to overcome these problems is through a greater number of social workers assigned and available to student athletes at high school and collegiate levels.

YOUTH SPORTS AND SOCIAL PROBLEMS

Young people are blank canvases molded by life experiences, mentors, social examples, and peers. Youth athletes are often perceived to be in need of intervention due to being at-risk, problematic, disadvantaged, lower class, or deprived (Haudenhuyse, Theeboom, & Coalter,

2012). Intervention strategies for young athletes often fail to grasp the complexities of social issues young athlete face and the problems are often vague and loosely applied to as majority issues rather than the individual. There is a need for a broader structure of social work for athletes and youth athletes, because society fails to tackle social problems at an early age and hardly take into account the importance of social intervention for young athletes (Haudenhuyse, et al., 2012). Youth athletes are one of the most socially vulnerable groups. Haudenhuyse and colleagues (2012) stated that "the theory of social vulnerability is the progressive accumulation of negative experiences with institutions of society such as family, school, labor market, healthcare, justice that eventually amount into social disconnectedness." Our social structure festers an environment for exclusion and discrimination processes; we tend to become stigmatized and self-perceived as incompetent due to lack of success resulting in our youth becoming exposed at a higher degree to social vulnerability (Haudenhuyse, et al., 2012). However, sports are viewed as the tool to alleviate distorted social relationships within an educational setting.

Teachers and coaches are held responsible for fixing the problem and also seen as enablers of positive social behavior. Yet, they both lack the training and professional background to manage such a massive responsibility. Social workers are one of the few professions that have a background in various social theories such as social vulnerability and have the professional knowledge to enable positive social behavior. Haudenhuyse and others (2012) found that sport programs that adopt a social worker approach that is person centered rather than sport centered is more effective than a sport program that is coach driven, which in turn adds value and success to the sport program. It has been argued that it is more possible and effective for social workers to learn sport skills related to coaching than it is for coaches to learn behavior and social science therapy skills. The inclusion of social workers in all sports can influence a successful working bond between coaches, teachers, and social workers providing young athletes with the abilities to experience lifelong coping skills and social success.

Haudenhuyse and others (2012) research found that it is important to provide an equally valued sports experience by doing the following: do not make a difference between the good and the not so good players; treat everybody the same; provide equal attention. When these things are not done the athlete is at risk of feeling incompetent, feeling like a failure, experience feelings of rejection, and develop low self-esteem. The state of mind of athletes is so fragile, that it is not feasible for teachers and coaches to be absent of error when they are responsible for hundreds of athletes at one time. Teachers and coaches have first contact with athletes and their positions require care and responsibility. Teachers and coaches are responsible for creating an environment of success without assistance or help from social behavior experts. Mazzer and Rickwood (2015) confirms that teachers and coaches are caring by nature and their duties includes a formal expectation of identifying athletes/students in need, but have limited guidelines and procedural training on assisting young people with social behavior issues. However, most teachers have some formal training compared to coaches with little to no formal behavior identification training.

It is imperative to provide coaches and teachers with assistance in carrying out promotion, prevention, and early intervention. Collegiate institution place pressure on themselves to handle all problems related to sports and sport participants without proper support to handle things that may arise. Often, athletes do not receive the help needed in their lives until the issue makes national news or the issue has potentially ruined the athletes career. Teachers and coaches deserves to be highlighted for their efforts and the impact they have on youths/athletes, but society has to highlight that there is an immense urgency to administer a new support system for collegiate institutions/schools, teachers, coaches, and athletes. Social workers would be a vital asset to this sector to bridge the helping gap.

FAMILY AND SOCIAL DYNAMICS

Athletes tend to become involved with their sport of preference at a very early age. Often, the sport is chosen by an influential party in the athlete's life. Parents tend to select the sport for the youth and place the child on a path of either becoming a professional athlete or fail in the attempt. Little is known about the dyadic and reciprocal interactions between parents and their youth athlete. However, parents have a tremendous influence, but a lot of research is more focused on the relationship of the athlete and the coach. Parents can negatively influence youth athlete, causing severe anxiety for the youth based on the parent's expectations (Kaye, Frith, & Vosloo, 2015). Parents are expecting their child to achieve the unreasonable, often raising a child to obtain a professional athletic career against all odds absent of statistical measures and chances.

Parenting pressures contribute to a more threatening sport performance environment (Kaye, et al., 2015). Parents teach their youth to win at all cost, and becoming a professional athlete is the pinnacle of success. The youth athletes are not taught that other careers are an option or that the objective is to obtain a college degree. Therefore, many young athletes have a one-track mind with their college career. Unfortunately, for African-American athlete's performance stresses are substantial and college degree objectives are not seen as an alternative. Many youth athletes fear that they may not live up to their parents' expectations causing an intense level of pressure, which increases performance anxiety. Youths are expected to be competent in their field and the competence is the central of achievement motivation (Kaye, et al., 2015). Still, they lack psychological social support that can be provided from a Sport Life Betterment Coach. This shows that there is a tremendous need for implementation of a social work and sports organization partnership such as developing and carrying out a program such as the Sport Life Association of Betterment, providing athletes with Sport Life Betterment Coaches.

Bystanders only see success or strive of the athlete, because there is little known about the dyadic and reciprocal interactions between family and the athlete, Sport Life Betterment Coaches are needed to review the relationships and make an educated professional assumption of things needed to improve, prevent, or resolve those relationship stressors. It is important to understand a person's history in order to understand their strives and dreams. Family structure has a tremendous influence on athletes and their performance and mental health. Still, research studies focus more on the coach and athlete dynamics. Social services in sports development would unfold family pressures that causes negative impact to youth athletes such as severe anxiety for the youth based on the parental expectations (Kaye, et al., 2015).

Family pressures contribute to a more threatening sport performance environment; many youth athletes fear that they may not live up to their parents' expectations causing an intense level of pressure, which increases performance anxiety. Youths are expected to be competent in their field and the competence is the central of achievement motivation (Kaye, et al., 2015). However, there is no professional in place to guide athletes in awareness of competence and that it is the central of achievement motivation. Again, Sport Life Betterment Coaches and the execution of the Sport Life Association of Betterment would see the process through.

Achievement goal theory implies that athletes attempt to demonstrate competence in achievement contexts from their parent's perspective; children may form perceptions of their parents' goals for them through exposure to that environment (Kaye, et al., 2015). Parent and child's close relationship can positively or negatively affect the psychological state of a youth athlete. Kaye and colleagues (2015) were able to show "that binary relationship transmission, a phenomenon in which one person's mindset increases distress or reduces positive effect in another person, is a common occurrence in close relationships in everyday life." Along with anxiety (negative thoughts, inability to concentrate, and disrupted attention), worry is one of the most distressing feelings felt by youth athletes; worry has been viewed as the primary cognitive concern for the consequence of failure, concentration disruption, nervousness, and tension (Kaye, et al., 2015).   Parent's displaced goals upon youth athletes causes extraordinary levels of achievement goals which correlated to prominent levels of worry, anxiety, and tension. Youth athletes worry that they may not live up to the odds that their parents have placed upon them. Parental strong-arming and stress placed upon an athlete may be magnified by his/her household structure. However, social services or assigned social workers to each athlete will uncover such dysfunctional stagnations and curtail issues that athletes face because of these type pressures.

Student athlete households are often stressful because a majority of them fall within a low-economic status. A vast majority of student athletes come from single parent homes, where the athlete is under stress to provide and succeed (Parent, et al., 2013). Single parent homes face eminent levels of stress and financial issues, and children in these homes tend to have behavioral or emotional problems. Single parents often live in poverty or suffer from financial hardships; poverty decreases positive parenting behaviors and increases negative parenting behaviors, which in turn might disrupt a child's development, causing emotional or behavioral problems (Zalewski et. al, 2012). This research shows that these issues must be addressed on a psycho-social level through social services, but are left untapped because society fails to recognize low-economical statuses of athletes. Social services are often viewed to help "regular impoverished people," not our superior sport heroes because we view them as being impoverished or in need of psycho-social assistance.

WOMEN IN SPORTS AND SOCIAL ISSUES

Race, gender, and ethnicity shapes a player's sport experience (Padgett, 2018). Women have an uphill battle in a male dominated arena of sports. In sports organizations, management and leadership positions, women are underrepresented compared to the general population (Wicker, Breuer, & Hanau, 2012). As early as seven years old, grades are more important to girls and boys tend to recognize sports as more important. In sports gender plays a large role when related to social problems. Women athletes deal with issues such as: eating disorders, anxiety, chronic pain, pressure to win, depression, racism, sexism, sexual orientation, and masculine stigmas. Women in sports challenge "social order," where women are expected to be housewives, domesticated, irrational thinkers, moral guardians, feminine, and subordinate (Padgett, 2017).

Padgett (2017) explain that developmental progression of sport socialization process deemed that parents have a considerable influence on behavior cues such as: "participating and doing well in sports, gender differences in sport ability, enjoyment, and perceived usefulness are evident, parents encourage sons more than they encourage daughters to be physically active." Padgett (2017) determined that women/girls who are better than the average guy in sports threatens the gender system. They are perceived intimidating and a threat, and treated less than stellar. Often, women successful in sports are labeled as lesbian even if they are not and lose their endorsements if they are outed, and often shunned by teammates if they are lesbian and bullied at times if they do not identify as lesbian (Padgett, 2017). Women athletes arc taunted with slurs and homophobic rants, and teasing about their sexual orientation during game play. Men deal with the same issues when talking about sexual orientation and homophobia in sports.

Multicultural women experience racism and sexism more, while nearly all women deal with social class issues in sports. This study recommends implementing a social work plan in sports to help educate athletes on the psychology effects of racism, homophobia, sexism, gender bias, etc. A greater social work presence in sports would allow women and men athletes suffering through these types of social issues with appropriate counseling, support, and coping abilities to overcome such tragic social problems.

ETHNICITY IN SPORTS AND SOCIAL ISSUES

Athletes have overcome major strides in race and race relations, but to date deal with pressing racial discrimination and inequality difficulties. Race and ethnicity are thought to be the same, but race is a way to classify and ethnicity is a way to organize the differences amongst people. In sports, there has to be an understanding of a distinguishing factor of race and ethnicity. Ethnicity in Sports (2018) defines ethnicity as cultural characteristics, including language, nationality, country of origin, and custom; and race describes the use of biological features, especially skin color. Stodolska, Shinew, and Gordon (2018) discovered that ethnic identities drive an increase in specific sports. Strong ethnical and racial identities in sports leads to certain sports being viewed as self-defining. Fans and spectators only see angry racial exchanges between players or each other at games, but that is just the surface of the problem. Anti-ethnical attitudes are embraced in sports, ignorance and mis-education of racial stereotypes are accepted. Yet, a majority of athletes are from a minority background. Society equivalates success of multicultural people in athletics as a reflection of their ethnicity rather than their ability.

The physicality of sports brings to light issues of race and racism; ethnicity and sports provides insight on the formation of identity, community and society (Ethinicity in Sports, 2018). African American athletes are assumed to be more aggressive and lack intelligence compared than their Caucasian teammates. Sports allows athletes to define who they are through ethnicity such as sport strengths, weakness, stereotypes, culture views, and cultural behaviors. Sports have provided minorities the platform to show not only performance, but pride and celebration. Ethnicity can also fuel negative perception for certain groups of people. If one group shows flair, flamboyance, and creativity, it is stereotypically viewed as blackness, but athletes who are controlled are more associated to whiteness.

Lack of ethnicity awareness in sports worsens stereotypes, biases, and misconceptions. According to Ethnicity in Sports (2018), in the Unites States, Canada, Australia, and Great Britain, the media minimizes the work ethic and discipline of athletes of color, and emphasize white athletes as having a natural ability, hard workers, and more intelligent with superior leadership abilities. Sports is used as a means of bringing people together but has and still pushes people apart. Sports have not eased ethnic tension or misunderstandings of culture; it has amplified racial tension, and ethnic differences (Ethnicity in Sports, 2018). A stronger social worker presence in sports will bring about education of ethnic difference, bridging the gap of understanding, awareness, bias, and reduce tension.

PRESSURES OF BEING AN ATHLETE

Athletes that play on a collegiate level face limited career options, due to shortfalls of exposure to other career choices, conflicting demands of the role of student and athlete, and deficiency of support managing career transition options (Scheyett, Dean, & Zeitlin, 2016). Athletes build numerous skills and strengths through their sports experiences, but they are failed on every level on how to tap into their skills and build a good career after sports. Social work is needed in sports development to provide athletes with the gap to recognize their abilities and build upon them later in life. Social workers must have focus and discipline and are often tasked with engaging and structuring communities; student-athletes would make great social workers and mentors for other student-athletes, which social work would be a great after sports life career choice for athletes (Scheyett, Dean, & Zeitlin., 2016).

However, student athletes generally have a fixed revolving schedule that consist of school, sports, and sleep, which often results in isolation from anything other than their respective sport (Scheyett, Dean, & Zeitlin., 2016). There is a connection barrier between the athlete and the outside world causing insufficient identification in forming proper career development strategies, hindering athletes from transitioning to the real world because of stress, difficulty with attaining employment, and lack of ability to envision a career outside of sports (Scheyett, Dean, & Zeitlin., 2016).

REALISTIC ODDS AND IMPROVING THE OUTCOMES

The athletes agree to go to the colleges believing it is the ticket to playing professionally; in actuality "less than two percent of NCAA basketball and football players go on to play in the NBA or NFL" (New, 2016). Parents and coaches are playing the lottery with young athlete's futures and the athletes are left with empty feelings of failure, self-loathing, no college degree, or the possibility of a career because they were set up to believe that the 2 percent NCAA to NBA/NFL statistic did not apply to them. Parents have the responsibility to educate their children better when it comes to becoming a professional athlete. However, college recruitment and staff should be held accountable for the approach taken to persuade these young athletes to play for their schools. New (2016) pointed out that African-American athletes and their families should demand that colleges take the academic pursuit of these athletes more seriously.

High school athletes and their parents envision being a part of professional sports, but fail to understand how unlikely this opportunity is for the average person (Price, 2010). There has been a surplus of information warning athletes and parents about how the odds are against the athlete. Yet, parents and athletes tend to focus on the impractical rather than the possible. The possible is academics. Academics are often ignored; athletes are passed along through middle school, high school and college. The blame is not solely placed on the athlete. Parents, coaches, and universities all contribute to the issue. However, the athlete is left without a college degree, little to no real education, no prospect of getting a real-world job, no trade school education, and topped off with shattered dreams of playing professionally (Price, 2010).

National Collegiate Athletic Association (NCAA) statistics show that high school basketball and football players have an extremely low chance of moving on to professional sports. There are over 156,000 senior male high school basketball players and only 44 will be drafted in to the National Basketball Association (NBA) after college (Price, 2010). According to Price (2010), only 32 women out of just over 127,000 females high school senior players will play professionally. Only 250 high school football players of just over 317,000 seniors will be drafted. You have a better chance pursuing a baseball career with over 600 NCAA athletes of the 6700 college seniors that will be drafted to play professional baseball (Price, 2017).

Percentage wise in baseball 9.1% of athletes will go pro, men's basketball 1.1%, women's basketball 0.9%, football 1.5%, men's Ice Hockey 5.6%, and men's soccer 1.4% (NCAA.org). The following statistics were provided (Sonny, 2014):

> Football for Men: 1,121,744 boys play high school football in the US
> 1 in 40 high school players will play in college

1 in 1,010 high school players will be drafted to the NFL
1 in 325 college players will be drafted in the NFL
Basketball for Men: 535,569 boys play high school basketball in the US
1 in 17 high school players will play in college
1 in 8,926 high school players will be drafted to the NBA
1 in 525 college players will be drafted in the NBA
Basketball for Women: 436,100 girls play high school basketball in the US
1 in 16 high school players will play in college
1 in 12,114 high school players will be drafted to the WNBA
1 in 766 college players will be drafted in the WNBA

These statistics provide parents and athletes with an uncomfortable truth. Price (2010) states, "It

is unrealistic to rely on the educational system to launch a professional sports career; the

numbers simply do not support it."

INJURY RATES AND FATAL STATISTICS

Sports are dangerous in general, there is always a risk for some form of injury, but

football is the one of the most fatal sports. Football is dangerous because it is a collision sport

with long term effects such as Chronic Traumatic Encephalopathy (CTE) a degenerative brain

disease found in athletes, military veterans, and others with a history of repetitive brain trauma.

Football can not only cause a fatal traumatic brain injury, but it often causes broken bones and

spinal cord injuries (Kucera, K., Yau, R. Register-Mihalik, J., Marshall, S., Thomas, L., Wolf, S.,

Cantu, Robert C., Mueller, F., and Guskiewicz, K., 2017). Kucera and colleagues (2017) found

that during 2005-2014, a total of 28 deaths occurred from traumatic brain and spinal cord injuries

among high school (24 deaths) and college football players (4 deaths), the majority of those

deaths happened during competition as a result of tackling or being tackled. There is a 90

percent chance or greater that the fatal injury was due to a subdural hematoma because of a

concussion within 4 weeks of the death or from second impact syndrome (in which a second

concussion occurs before a first concussion has properly healed, causing rapid and severe brain swelling) (Kucera, et al., 2017). Fatal injuries are most common for running backs (32% of players overall) and linebackers (21%) (Kucera, et al., 2017).

In the United Stated over 30 million children and teens participate in some form of organized sports resulting in more than 3.5 million injuries occurring each year (Stanford Health, 2017). One-third of all injuries incurred in childhood are sports-related injuries; the most common injuries are sprains and strains (Stanford Health, 2017).

The following statistics are from the National SAFE KIDS Campaign and the American Academy of Pediatrics (Stanford Children Health, 2017):

INJURY RATES

More than 3.5 million children ages 14 and younger get hurt annually playing sports or participating in recreational activities.
Although, death from a sports injury is rare, the leading cause of death from a sports-related injury is a brain injury.

Sports and recreational activities contribute to approximately 21 percent of all traumatic brain injuries among American children.

Almost 50 percent of head injuries sustained in sports or recreational activities occur during bicycling, skateboarding, or skating incidents.

More than 775,000 children, ages 14 and younger, are treated in hospital emergency rooms for sports-related injuries each year. Most of the injuries occurred as a result of falls, being struck by an object, collisions, and overexertion during unorganized or informal sports activities.

TYPES OF SPORTS AND RECREATIONAL ACTIVITIES
Consider these estimated injury statistics for 2009 from the Consumer Product Safety Commission (Stanford Children Health, 2017):

Basketball. More than 170,000 children ages 5 to 14 were treated in hospital emergency rooms for basketball-related injuries.

Baseball and softball. Nearly 110,000 children ages 5 to 14 were treated in hospital emergency rooms for baseball-related injuries. Baseball also has the highest fatality rate among sports for children ages 5 to 14, with three to four children dying from baseball injuries each year.

Bicycling. More than 200,000 children ages 5 to 14 were treated in hospital emergency rooms for bicycle-related injuries.

Football. Almost 215,000 children ages 5 to 14 were treated in hospital emergency rooms for football-related injuries.

Ice hockey. More than 20,000 children ages 5 to 14 were treated in hospital emergency rooms for ice hockey-related injuries.

In-line and roller skating. More than 47,000 children ages 5 to 14 were treated in hospital emergency rooms for in-line skating-related injuries.

Skateboarding. More than 66,000 children ages 5 to 14 were treated in hospital emergency rooms for skateboarding-related injuries.

Sledding or toboggan. More than 16,000 children ages 5 to 14 were treated in hospital emergency rooms for sledding-related injuries.

Snow skiing or snowboarding. More than 25,000 children ages 5 to 14 were treated in hospital emergency rooms for snow-boarding and snow skiing-related injuries.

Soccer. About 88,000 children ages 5 to 14 were treated in hospital emergency rooms for soccer-related injuries.

Trampolines. About 65,000 children ages 14 and under were treated in hospital emergency rooms for trampoline-related injuries.

On average 1.7 percent of college football players and 0.08 percent of high school players play any professional sport (Uhlmann, E. & Barnes, 2014). Yet, professional sports are idolized and has become top priority over completing a college degree, obtaining a trade or skill, and getting a regular job (i.e. information technology specialist, lawyer, any type of licensed professional, business owner). Increased salary caps, sports celebrities, endorsers, advertisers, coaches, parents, colleges, team owners, and leagues are encouraging and promoting the lavish life of sports to increase revenue, but at the cost of a realistic future for youth athletes. Particularly, African-American male youths' futures are lost in the promotion of sales, increase in revenue, and lack of knowledge of statistical odds of becoming a professional athlete. African-American male athletes are completing college at significantly lower rates than athletes of different ethnicities (Thomas & Nasir, 2013). Due to a lack of a college degree, trade or skill and no plan B, this group of men tend to return home and back to an impoverished environment. Poverty may often lead to crime and combined together, both leave people with two choices:

either take part in criminal activities or try to find legal but quite limited sources of income (Ward, 2015).

This research seeks to empower all athletes, promote the completion of college degrees and promote the importance of learning a trade or skill with the placement of social workers in collegiate/school systems. All while enlightening parents, coaches, and institutions on an immediate need for behavioral change amongst them. This research and the understanding of the drastic need for social workers in sports, would lead to possible restoration of the importance of academic learning in the African-American community (Marsh, Darity, Cohen, Casper & Salters, 2007). The results of the dyadic relational study show that African-American athletes' graduation rates can increase with realistic achievement goals set by parents, different performance goals set by coaches, and institutional changes within colleges, and help all athletes find a better after sports life on a collegiate level or a professional level.

The pressure to win at all cost needs to be changed from a parental and coaching perspective because professional careers are short and immensely unlikely to achieve. Athletes should be burdened to graduate college at any cost, obtain a college degree, learn a trade, beat the odds of graduating college rather than fighting the unrealistic odds of playing on a professional level. Displaced performance stress from coaches results in athletes focusing on the coach's approval rather than the actual goal of attending college, which is to graduate with a college degree not graduate to a professional sport. Displaced achievement goals are a result of parents placing their youth athlete in a position to fail without providing the child with real life statistics and realistic life goals. Parental achievement goals and expectations should be placed on completing college rather than on obtaining a professional sports career. Minority athletes' graduation rates would rise and their after sports life would improve. It is imperative that college institutions place more attention on academics rather than profits or pay equal attention to both. Academics should be just as important as profits in a college environment.

CONCLUSION

O'Rourke, Smith, Smoll, and Cumming (2014) found empirical evidence that proved both parents and coaches influence the psychosocial well-being of children and youths in sports. Parents and coaches influence perception, attitude, values, beliefs, motivation, emotions, self-esteem, competitive spirit, and moral development (O'Rourke, et al., 2014). In order to change the game and the future of all athletes and increase their college graduation rate and maintain a better after sports life, there has to be intervention and studies that alter the behavior of parents and coaches. Intervention studies have proven to show that young athletes can benefit through changes in adult behavior in a variety of domains, including self-esteem, anxiety, sport attrition reduction, and achievement goal orientation (O'Rourke, et al., 2014). A program such as Sport Life Association of Betterment implementing the cycle of policy research process in athletes for the lack of social services in sports would be the intervention study that O'Rourke and colleagues (2014) research validates.

Sadly, there are cases where adults take advantage of mentoring young athletes resulting in the occurrence of sexual abuse at the hands of coaches, administrators, school authority figures, and teachers. Coaches and teachers are hesitant to report colleagues and there is hardly any empirical evidence on how to help them manage these accusations or suspicions when they occur. Social workers are usually called upon in times of distress and trauma (Levenson, 2017). Athletes are rarely viewed as individuals that deal with the type of trauma that needs the help of a social worker. However, social workers would be beneficial to athletic departments. Research and literature on how to protect student-athletes against sexual abuse is nonexistent. A strong social worker presence in this sector would curtail the problem. Trauma at an early age can shape how an individual views the world and affects his or her psychosocial behavior during their life time.

Social workers are trained to deliver services such as: core principles of safety, trust collaboration, choice, and empowerment while educating clients on how to avoid unhealthy interpersonal relationship dynamics (Levenson, 2017). Social worker presence on university campuses can help address mental abuse, sexual abuse, and physical abuse within athletic departments. Social worker presence can build a foundation for athletes making sound educated decisions on preparing for an after-sports life and coping with the pressure of being an athlete. There is a substantial need for research, education, and awareness in this area along with a social workers presence to aid in identifying signs, symptoms, and procedures for reporting sexual abuse between authority figures in youth athletics (Teasley and Gill, 2015).

Social work is geared toward individual needs when handled on a local and state level. There are areas where family and preservation are concerned, but it is focused on the empowerment of an individual. Cultural development in social work can lead to community development, then it will successfully address individual development. Society only pays attention when the problem of the individual has become so grand it is almost impossible to wrangle the issue and restore order and peace. The lack of social workers in sports development is becoming and has become so enormous that we are nearly at the point of no return and leaving this vulnerable group to fend for themselves, which is detrimental to society as a whole.

FUTURE RESEARCH

Social work in sports development future research projects should attempt to explore the relationship between social services, sport participation, and academics; study the life experience of student athletes and social services and how the services contributed to improving coping skills and a better after sports life; explore the social conditions for positive effects of social work in sports development, and provide insight on how social workers, coaches, parents, and scholarly facilities can best collaborate (Hermens, 2017). I plan to conclude this theoretical idea and Heir to the Invisible Throne Syndrome: Sports Development and the American Dream with a research proposal and dissertation comparing and linking social work and sport for development by analyzing the purpose, processes and outcome of sport for development in relation to social work.

References

Aldridge, D. (2018). NBA, NBPA taking steps to further address mental wellness issues for players. Retrieved from http://www.nba.com/article/2018/03/12/morning-tip-nba-nbpa addressing-mental-wellness-issues

Bertram, V. (2013). Pursue Your Dreams, Prepare for Reality. Retrieved from https://www.huffingtonpost.com/vince-bertram/pursue-your-dreams stem_b_4704090.html.

Bromfield, R. (2008). On your own. *Scholastic Parent & Child.* 15 (5), 56-57.

Brown, S., Garvey, T., Harden, T. (2011). A sporting chance: Exploring the connection between social work with groups and sports for at-risk urban youth. *Groupwork*, 21 (3), 62-77. DOI: 10.1921/095182411X636563.

Crabbe, T. (2000). A Sporting Chance?: using sport to tackle drug use and crime. *Drugs: education, prevention and policy*, 7 (4), 381-391.

Engard, B. (2017). 5 Social Work Theories That Inform Practice. Retrieved from https://online.campbellsville.edu/social-work/social-work-theories/

Greville, L. (2014). Sports can be great learning experiences, but student athletes with behavioral health issues may be overlooked in the quest to win. *Social Work Today*, 14 (4), 22.

Gill Jr., Emmett L. (2008). Mental Health in College Athletics: It's Time for Social Work to get in the Game. *Social Work*, 53 (1), 85-88.

Haudenhuyse, R. P., Theeboom, M., & Coalter, F. (2012). The potential of sports based social interventions for vulnerable youth: implications for sport coaches and youth workers. *Journal of Youth Studies,* 15 (4), 437-454. DOI: 10.1080/13676261.2012.663895.

Hermens, N., De Langen, L., Verkooijen, K, & Koelen, M. (2017). Co-ordinated action between youth-care and sports: facilitators and barriers. *Health and Social Care in the Community, 25*(4), 1318–1327. DOI: 10.1111/hsc.12431.

Kaye, M., Frith, A., & Vosloo, J. (2015). Dyadic anxiety in youth sport: The relationship of achievement goals with anxiety in young athletes and their parents. *Journal of Applied Sport Psychology, 27*, 171-185.

Kucera, K., Yau, R. Register-Mihalik, J., Marshall, S., Thomas, L., Wolf, S., Cantu, Robert C., Mueller, F., & Guskiewicz, K. (2017). Traumatic Brain and Spinal Cord Fatalities Among High School and College Football Players — United States, 2005–2014. MMWR: Morbidity & Mortality Weekly Report. 65 (52), 1469. DOI: 10.15585/mmwr.mm6552a2.

Larsen, C. H., Alfermann, D., Henriksen, K., & Christensen, M. K. (2014). Preparing Footballers for the Next Step: An Intervention Program From an Ecological Perspective. *Sport Psychologist, 28*(1), 91-102. doi:10.1123/pes.2013-0015

Levenson, J. (2017). Trauma-Informed Social Work Practice. *Social Work*, 62 (2), DOI: 10.1093/sw/swx001.

Mazzer, K. R., Rickwood, D. J. (2015). Teachers' and coaches' role perceptions for supporting young people's mental health: Multiple group path analyses. *Australian Journal of Psychology*, 67(1), 10-19. DOI: 10.1111/ajpy.12055.

NASWIS (2017). Alliance of Social Workers in Sports. Retrieved from https://www.naswis.org/

New, J. (2016). Racial Gaps in the Power 5. Inside Higher Education. Retrieved from

>https://www.insidehighered.com/news/2016/03/16/black-athletes-wealthiest-conferences

>continue-graduate-low-rates.

Noren, N. (2014, January 22). Taking notice of hidden injury. Retrieved

>from http://espn.go.com/espn/otl/story/_/id/10335925/awareness-better-treatment

>college-athletes-mental-health-begins-take-shape.

O'Rourke, D., Smith, R., Smoll, F., & Cumming, S. (2014). Relations of Parent- and Coach-

>initiated motivational climates to young athletes' self-esteem, performance anxiety, and

>autonomous motivation: Who is more influential? Journal of Applied Sport Psychology,

>26, 395-408; DOI: 10.1080/10413200.2014.907838.

Padgett, J. (2017). Issues of Women in Sports. Retrieved on April 24, 2018 from

>serendip.brynmawr.edu/local/scisoc/sports02/papers/jpadgett.html

Parent, J., Jones, D., Forehand, R., Cuellar, J. & Shoulberg, E. (2013). The Role of Co-parents in

>African American Single-Mother Families: The Indirect Effect of Co-parent Identity on

>Youth Psychosocial Adjustment. *Journal of Family Psychology, 27 (2)*, 252-262. DOI:

>10.1037/a0031477.

Price, W. (2010). What Are the Odds of Becoming a Professional Athlete? *The Sports Digest*.

>Retrieved fromhttp://www.thesportdigest.com/archive/article/what-are-odds-becoming

>professional-athlete.

Scheyett, A., Dean, C., & Zeitlin, L. (2016). Strength and Motivation: What College Athletes

>Bring to Social Work. Journal of Teaching in Social Work, 36 (3), 312-325. DOI:

>10.1080/08841233.2016.1185077.

Simmons School of Social Work (2014). Theories Used in Social Work Practice & Practice

Models. Retrieved from https://socialwork.simmons.edu/theories-used-social-work

practice/.

Sonny, J. (2014). The Statistical Breakdown of Becoming A Professional Athlete Will Make

You Keep Your Day Job. Retrieved from https://www.elitedaily.com/sports/odds-going

pro-sports-will-make-rethink-day-job.

Stanford Children Health (2017). Sports Injury Statistics. Retrieved from http://www.stanford

childrens.org/en/topic/default?id=sports-injury-statistics-90-P02787.

Stodolska, M., Shinew, M.F., Gordon, W. (2018). Race, Ethnicity, and Leisure. Sport

participation and the effect on one's identity. Retrieved on April 25, 2018 from

http://www.humankinetics.com/excerpts/excerpts/sport-participation-and-the

effect-on-onersquos-identity.

Teasley, M. L. & Gill, E. (2015). School Sports, Sexual Abuse, and the Utility of School Social=

Workers. Children & Schools, 37 (1), 4-7.

The College of St. Scholastica (2017). Social workers in sports: Support the well-being of

athletes. Retrieved on April 24, 2018 from http://www.css.edu/the-sentinel-blog/social

workers-in-sports-support-the-well-being-of-athletes.html.

Thomas, I., & Nasir, N. (2013). Black males, athletes and academic achievement. *Huffington

Post*. Retrieved from http://www.huffingtonpost.com/isiah-thomas/black-males-athletes

and-_b_3232989.html.

Thompson, M., Dieffenbach, K., (2016). Measuring Professional Ethics in Coaching:

Development of the PISC-Q. *Ethics & Behavior*, 26 (6), 507-523. DOI:

10.1080/10508422.2015.1060578.

Uhlmann, E. & Barnes, C. (2014). Selfish play increases during high-stakes NBA games and is rewarded with more lucrative contracts. *PLoS ONE, 9* (4), 1-5. DOI: 10.1371/journal.pone.0095745.

Ward, M. (2015). Poverty and Crime. Retrieved from http://www.nationaldialoguenetwork org/poverty-and-crime/.

Wicker, P., Breuer, C., & Hanau, T., (2012). Gender Effects on Organizational Problems Evidence from Non-Profit Sports Clubs in Germany. *Sex Roles*. 66 (1-2), 105-116. DOI: 10.1007/s11199-011-0064-8.

Zalewski, M., Lengua, L., Fisher, P., Trancik, A., Bush, N. & Meltzoff, A., (2012). Poverty and single parenting: Relations with preschoolers' cortisol and effortful control. *Infant & Child Development*. 21 (5), 537-554. DOI: 10.1002/icd.1759.

www.ingramcontent.com/pod-product-compliance
Lightning Source LLC
Chambersburg PA
CBHW080046260726
48658CB00007B/2770